Look, There's a Hippopotamus in the Playground Eating Cake

Look, There's a HIPPOPOTAMUS in the Playground Eating Cake

by Hazel Edwards

illustrated by Deborah Niland

PUFFIN BOOKS

For Garnet and for my friend Aileen
H.E.

For all children and hippopotamuses
D.N.

PUFFIN BOOKS

UK | USA | Canada | Ireland | Australia
India | New Zealand | South Africa | China

Penguin Books is part of the Penguin Random House group of companies
whose addresses can be found at global.penguinrandomhouse.com.

Penguin
Random House
Australia

First published by Hodder Headline Australia Pty Ltd (a member of the Hodder Headline Group), 1994
First published by Penguin Group (Australia), 2006
This edition published by Penguin Random House Pty Ltd, 2017

Text copyright © Hazel Edwards, 1994.
Illustrations copyright © Deborah Niland, 1994.
The moral right of the author and illustrator has been asserted.

Offset from the Hodder Headline edition.
Colour separation by Splitting Image Colour Studio, Clayton, Victoria.
Printed and bound in China.

National Library of Australia Cataloguing-in-Publication data is available for this book.

penguin.com.au

Ouch!
Ouch!
Ouch!
My new shoes hurt.

My mummy says the shoes fit.
My hippopotamus doesn't think so.
Clunk.
Clunk.
Clunk.
There's a hippopotamus tiptoeing
on our roof eating cake.

My daddy asks if any of my friends are starting school too.
I shake my head.
But I have a Special Friend.
He's the hippopotamus on our roof eating cake.
And he might go to school with me.

My hippopotamus doesn't really need to go to school.
He knows everything.
He knows all about
chocolate cake
carrot cake
ice-cream cake
and birthday cake!
But he might be lonely without me.
So my hippopotamus is going to school too.

Mummy made my paint smock.
Daddy made my sandwiches.
I've got a new school bag.
I put my red drink bottle and my red lunch box in
my school bag.
My hippopotamus is packing his school bag too.

'Goodbye,' Mummy kissed me.
'Goodbye,' Daddy kissed me.
I didn't want to say 'Goodbye' to my hippopotamus.
So he came with me.
School children look very big.
I'm glad my hippopotamus came too.

We line up.
Miss Lee tells us what to do.
'Hang your bags on the pegs, children.'
Mummy put name tags on all of my things.
My hippopotamus has a name tag on his cake.

Miss Lee asks us to draw something on the chalkboard.
I draw a red hippopotamus with red chalk.
The boy next to me draws a blue elephant with blue chalk. The boy's name is Sam.
My hippopotamus draws a huge cake with lots of different colours.

At playtime we play hide-and-seek.
There are lots of places to hide.
My hippopotamus isn't scared of the big kids.
He hides really well.

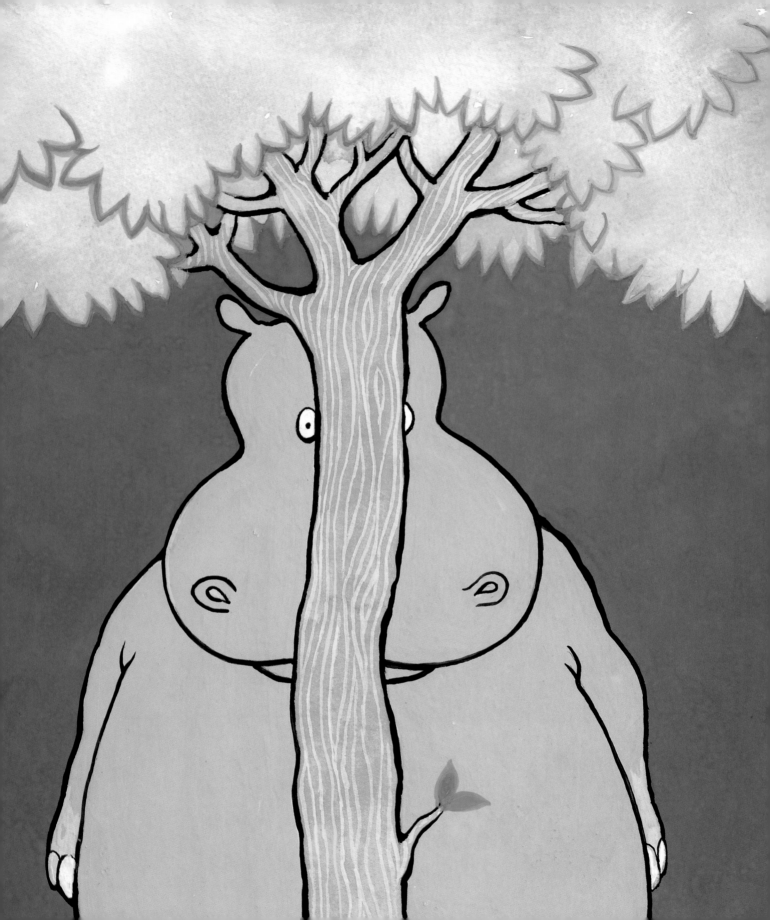

At lunchtime I take out my lunch box.
I eat my salad sandwiches.
I eat my apple.
I drink my juice.
But my hippopotamus sits on the
school roof and eats cake.

The playground is fun.
The slippery slide is very up and down.
The swings go very high.
But my hippopotamus likes the monkey bars best.

Our classroom has tables and chairs.
My hippopotamus sits on top of the cupboards.
Until Miss Lee opens the door and everything falls out.

We all sit on the mat.
The mat is green and orange.
Sam sits next to me.
Miss Lee tells us an animal story.
My hippopotamus listens from the window
of our classroom.

Afterwards Sam asks, 'Do you want to play?'
We have good fun until home time.
At teatime Daddy asks, 'How was school?'
'I've got a new friend,' I tell him.

Tomorrow my hippopotamus might want to stay home
on the roof
eating cake.